For my incredible wife Ange-Marie who inspires me every day, and my wonderful parents and family that support me in every way.

– Stephen

To my extraordinary wife Katie for every ounce of support she's given me.

– Kyle

the magic poof

Stephen Hodges

Illustrated by
T. Kyle Gentry

To order additional copies of this book, contact: Xlibris Corporation
1-888-795-4274   www.Xlibris.com   Orders@Xlibris.com

Ange-Marie always felt different.

There was her name, pronounced AAHHNGE=Marie...... and then there was the Poof.

The Poof sprang up as a great ball of curly hair that sat on top of Ange-Marie's head.

When she walked, it bounced.

When she skipped, it bounded.

And when she danced, it boogied.

Even after a haircut the Poof would still be there.

The Poof was alive of course. And he had a wild personality!
"What'cha eatin' down there?" the Poof would ask Ange-Marie over breakfast.

"What's that thing?" he'd quiz, pointing to different objects around the room.

"Look! I'm a balloon!" he'd exclaim, while floating to the ceiling with Ange-Marie attached.

"When are we going to plaaaayyyy???"
he'd whine as Ange-Marie brushed her teeth.

"Not now." she said. "I'm busy you see."

"Doing what?" the Poof asked, forming into a giant question mark.

"No wait . . . I want to be . . . Not so fluffy."
he thought, shrinking down into a tiny little ball.

"Not so fluffy . . ."

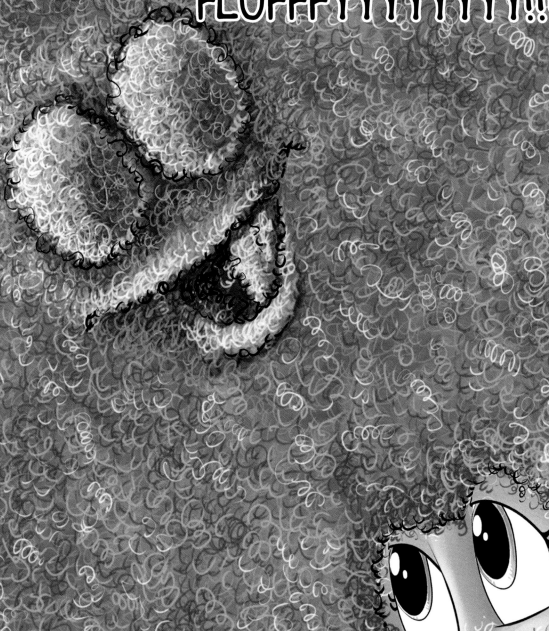

The Poof was acting nutty. He just didn't know what he wanted to be for picture day.

"But you can't be one or the other," said Ange-Marie, "You have to look like my normal hair."

"Ohhh, but I don't like keeping our secret," the Poof pouted, "I want to be me!"

"I know. But most people don't know about Magic Poofs, and if they found out, they might not understand. Pleeeaassee????"

The Poof could never resist Ange-Marie's "please." "Ohh, ok, your smile always gets me."

He formed into Ange-Marie's normal hair and off they went.

The pair arrived at school and entered the room where the photographer was setting up his camera. "I'll just be a minute," he said and turned away.

The Poof tapped Ange-Marie on the shoulder and whispered in her ear.

"Can't I be something for picture day?" he begged. "Fluffy...? Not so fluffy...? I still want to be me. Pleeeaassee????"

"Ohh, Ok." Ange-Marie grinned. She couldn't resist the Poof's "please" either. "Just don't give away our secret."

The Poof bobbed happily in agreement.

The photographer turned and said
"Ready? Ok, Smile!"

With a click and a flash the picture was taken and a barely visible smile appeared in the Poof's curls.

Even the photographer thought he saw Ange-Marie's hair grinning, but that was impossible!

After school ended, the twosome happily headed home.

"This is one of my favorite pictures of us!"
Ange-Marie laughed.

The Poof had to agree. He bounced up and down and beamed the
biggest smile she had ever seen her hair make.

They both agreed. It was truly wonderful to be attached to your best friend.

Edwards Brothers Malloy
Thorofare, NJ USA
August 29, 2016